SLACK KEY GUITAR

THE G KILAUEA TUNING

Published by:
Daniel Ho Creations
914 Westwood Boulevard #813
Los Angeles, California 90024
www.DanielHo.com

Written by Daniel Ho

Edited by Lydia Miyashiro

Photography by Lydia Miyashiro
and Daniel Ho

Graphic layout by Sharlene Oshiro

Historical sources: Steve Sano
and Dancing Cat Productions

Artistic photos of Yamaha guitar
by Kate Killian.

Ocean cover photo taken from
Outrigger Waikiki Hotel.

Daniel Ho plays Yamaha guitars.

Table of Contents

Origin & Evolution
of Hawaiian Slack Key Guitar

In 1832, the first *vaqueros*, cowboys from Mexico, arrived on the Big Island of Hawai'i. They were invited by King Kamehameha III to teach Hawaiians how to manage their cattle. The *vaqueros* brought guitars with them and taught the *paniolo*, Hawaiian cowboys, how to play. The *paniolo* eventually developed their own unique tunings and music style known today as *ki ho'alu*, or Hawaiian slack key guitar.

Slack key is played on regular guitars with certain strings slackened from standard tuning (E A D G B E). Tunings were created to allow guitarists to play in different keys, accommodate vocal ranges, and facilitate distinctive musical phrases. Historically, slack key tunings were closely guarded family secrets. Due to its recent surge in popularity, information about slack key tunings is now readily available. There are hundreds of slack key tunings, but what emerged as the most recognized is the *G Taro Patch* tuning (D G D G B D).

A New Musical Voice

It was almost a decade ago and I remember it vaguely. I was on a month-long U.S. tour playing keyboards in the pit orchestra of a theatrical circus show. It was a circus, both literally and figuratively. As an artist, I was transitioning from one genre to another—contemporary jazz to Hawaiian—from piano to guitar. I was balancing my personal and financial responsibilities against my elusive quest for a new musical voice. With my travel guitar in hand, I searched and searched—on the tour bus, waiting at the airport, in the hotel room, at soundcheck. I can't remember if it was on the 10-hour bus ride to Schenectady, or in a Cincinnati hotel room when it came to me, but I am ever so grateful it did. In recognition of the contemporary jazz band that I toured and recorded with for the prior six years, I named my discovery the *G Kilauea* tuning.

I have been using this tuning since 1998 for almost all of my fingerstyle guitar playing. I have experimented with other tunings, but found the *G Kilauea* tuning to be the most versatile and functional for solo instrumentals and vocal accompaniment.

The Best of Both Worlds

The *G Kilauea* tuning is a hybrid of standard tuning and the *G Taro Patch* tuning. It combines the best of both worlds: the fullness of *G Taro Patch* and the flexibility of standard tuning. In Hawaiian music, it is classified as a *Ho'opa'a* tuning, where at least one string needs to be fretted by the left hand to make a chord.

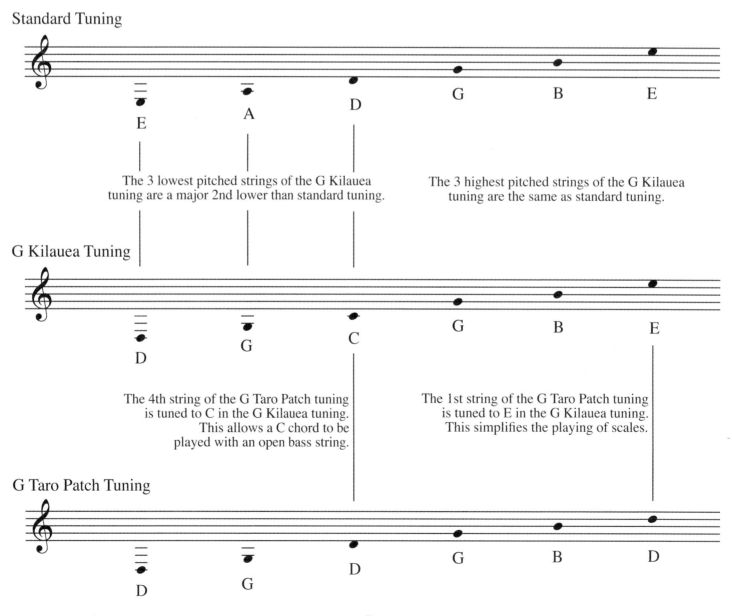

Standard Tuning

E A D G B E

The 3 lowest pitched strings of the G Kilauea tuning are a major 2nd lower than standard tuning.

The 3 highest pitched strings of the G Kilauea tuning are the same as standard tuning.

G Kilauea Tuning

D G C G B E

The 4th string of the G Taro Patch tuning is tuned to C in the G Kilauea tuning. This allows a C chord to be played with an open bass string.

The 1st string of the G Taro Patch tuning is tuned to E in the G Kilauea tuning. This simplifies the playing of scales.

G Taro Patch Tuning

D G D G B D

Six Principles for Six Strings

Mathematically, the six strings of a guitar can be tuned to 2,985,984 combinations (each string has 12 different notes: $12^6 = 2,985,984$). Practically, here are six principles that simplify the process of finding a tuning. Each principle is followed by explanations on how they were used to form the *G Kilauea* tuning.

String Tension

A guitar is designed to function best in standard tuning (E A D G B E). Changing the tension of the strings disrupts the delicate balance of the instrument. It affects the curvature of the neck and the action (height of the strings above the fretboard). Selecting pitches too far from standard tuning can compromise the accuracy of the intonation, make the guitar difficult to play, or cause the strings to buzz. A minor third below or a major second above standard tuning is an acceptable range. Increasing a guitar's overall string tension will produce a brighter, snappier sound, which often works well for up-tempo pieces. Reducing string tension makes a guitar sound fuller and warmer, a suitable sound for slower pieces.

The three highest pitched strings of the *G Kilauea* tuning: G, B, and E, remain in standard tuning. The three lowest pitched strings: D, G, and C, are tuned down a whole step, but still within a minor third of standard tuning. The result is a richer and deeper sound.

Key

Slack key tunings are generally in major keys because they were created to play Hawaiian music, which is almost always in major tonalities. If a song is in a minor key, consider designing a tuning to suit that key. For example, the *G Taro Patch* tuning is a G major chord (D G D G B D), which makes playing in G minor a challenge. By lowering the B to Bb, *G Taro Patch* becomes a G minor chord ((D G D G Bb D).

Similar to standard tuning, the *G Kilauea* tuning functions well in both major and minor keys. This versatility has its advantages in live performance as it eliminates the need to retune between songs.

Open Strings

The primary objective of alternate tunings is to increase the number of open strings available in a piece. A guitar sounds most resonant when the full lengths of the strings are vibrating. Open strings contribute to a rich tone full of sympathetic vibrations and overtones that are not as prominent when strings are shortened by fretting with the left hand. When the left hand is not required to finger many notes or bar chords, it is free to play more intricate parts. The sustain of open strings also helps to smoothen chord transitions.

The *G Kilauea* tuning maximizes the number of playable open strings by providing three bass notes: D, G, and C, and a common tone on the 3rd string: G.

Melody

Melodies are usually played on the top three strings of a guitar, and occasionally on the lower strings. Imagine the guitar as an orchestra—the highest pitched strings (like a violin section) play the melody, the middle strings (violas and celli) cover the harmony, and the lowest strings (string basses) play bass notes. Of course, with only six strings, the sections overlap.

The top three strings of the *G Kilauea* tuning: G, B, and E, are the same as standard tuning. Major, minor, and pentatonic scales can be played without changing left hand positions. This makes it ideal for melodies. In the *G Taro Patch* tuning, the top string (1st string) is tuned to D, which requires a position change to play a scale.

Harmony

This function is assigned to the 2nd, 3rd, and 4th strings of a guitar, with an emphasis on the 3rd string. Tuning strings to common tones of frequently used chords relieves the left hand of carrying out harmonic tasks, and affords it the freedom to phrase melodies anywhere on the fingerboard.

As stated above, the 3rd string of the *G Kilauea* tuning: G, is a common tone in both the G chord (I chord in the key of G) and the C chord (IV chord in the key of G). This is a valuable facet of the *G Kilauea* tuning. In standard tuning, E, A, and D are common keys because they utilize many open strings. However, the high E string (1st string) is the common tone in these keys—it is the root of an E chord, the 5th of an A chord, and the 9th of a D chord. Since melodies are played on the highest strings, the 1st string is not viable as a common tone. The *G Kilauea* tuning repositions the common tone to the 3rd string, allowing the 1st and 2nd strings to serve their melodic function. As a result, much of the harmony is defined without fingering the 3rd string. It allows the left hand to focus on the phrasing and expression of the melody.

Bass

Bass notes occupy the 4th, 5th, and 6th strings of a guitar. Tuning these strings to the most commonly used bass notes will allow the left hand to move freely across the neck. Given that bass notes are low pitches, they are heard as fundamentals and should be spaced at the most consonant intervals possible. This will help them to blend into each other's overtones and avoid obvious dissonances when they sound together. Pianists often play octaves, fifths and fourths with the left hand while playing chords with the right hand. This is because in the overtone series, the octave is the first interval above the fundamental (most consonant), a perfect fifth is the second interval (less consonant), and a perfect fourth is the third interval (even less consonant).

Overtone Series based on a G fundamental

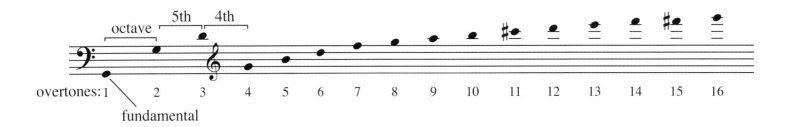

The *G Kilauea* tuning addresses these considerations by assigning the I, IV and V bass notes in the key of G as open strings. The I, IV, and V chords are perhaps the most frequently used chords in music. The 6th string is tuned to D (the root of the V chord in the key of G), the 5th string is tuned to G (the root of the I chord in the key of G), and the 4th string is tuned to C (the root of the IV chord in the key of G). D is a perfect 4th (the third most consonant interval) from G, G is a perfect 4th from C, and all three strings are within the range of an octave. Keeping these pitches within the range of an octave preserves their function as a bass section. If the 6th, 5th, and 4th strings were tuned to C, G, and D respectively, they would span an interval of a 9th, making the D (a 9th above the low C) sound like part of the harmony instead of the bass.

The *G Taro Patch* tuning does not represent the root of the IV chord, C, as an open string. The left hand is required to finger the 5th fret of the 5th string to produce a C bass note. This restricts the left hand to the 5th position on the neck when playing a IV chord. The three lowest strings in standard tuning contain the roots of the V (E), I (A), and IV (D) chords in the key of A. However, the 3rd string, G, is not in the key of A; and the common tone, E, is on the 1st string where melodies are played.

G Kilauea Fretboard

This diagram illustrates the position of each note on the fretboard in the *G Kilauea* tuning. To be fluent and creative in this tuning, it would help to be familiar with this chart.

D	C#/Db	C	B	A#/Bb	A	G#/Ab	G	F#/Gb	F	E	D#/Eb	
G	F#/Gb	F	E	D#/Eb	D	C#/Db	C	B	A#/Bb	A	G#/Ab	D
C	B	A#/Bb	A	G#/Ab	G	F#/Gb	F	E	D#/Eb	D	C#/Db	G
G	F#/Gb	F	E	D#/Eb	D	C#/Db	C	B	A#/Bb	A	G#/Ab	C
B	A#/Bb	A	G#/Ab	G	F#/Gb	F	E	D#/Eb	D	C#/Db	C	G
E	D#/Eb	D	C#/Db	C	B	A#/Bb	A	G#/Ab	G	F#/Gb	F	B
												E

G Major Scale

While the *G Kilauea* tuning is also quite functional in the keys of C and D, this book will focus on the key of G major, for which this tuning was designed. All melodies, chords and bass notes in the key of G are derived from the G major scale. The degrees of the scale indicate the note's relationship to the tonal center, or key of G.

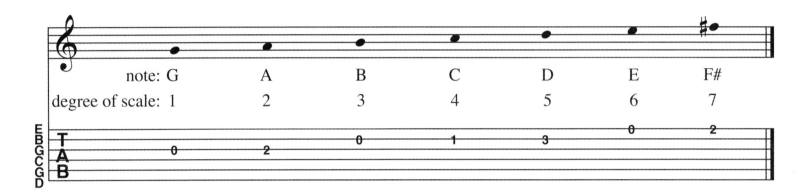

note:	G	A	B	C	D	E	F#
degree of scale:	1	2	3	4	5	6	7

The black dots in the following diagram map out the G major scale in the *G Kilauea* tuning.

D	C#/Db	C	B	A#/Bb	A	G#/Ab	G	F#/Gb	F	E	D#/Eb	
G	F#/Gb	F	E	D#/Eb	D	C#/Db	C	B	A#/Bb	A	G#/Ab	G
C	B	A#/Bb	A	G#/Ab	G	F#/Gb	F	E	D#/Eb	D	C#/Db	C
G	F#/Gb	F	E	D#/Eb	D	C#/Db	C	B	A#/Bb	A	G#/Ab	G
B	A#/Bb	A	G#/Ab	G	F#/Gb	F	E	D#/Eb	D	C#/Db	C	B
E	D#/Eb	D	C#/Db	C	B	A#/Bb	A	G#/Ab	G	F#/Gb	F	E

G Major Pentatonic Scale

Particularly effective for improvisation, the G major pentatonic scale eliminates the leading tones, C (the 4th degree) and F# (the 7th degree), of the G major scale. Leading tones require resolution: the C "leads" down to B (the 3rd degree), and the F# "leads" up to G (the tonic or 1st degree). C to B and F# to G are also the only half-step intervals in the G scale. By excluding leading tones, the G major pentatonic scale avoids a major scale's natural tendencies to resolve. It also prevents the potential dissonances of half-step intervals. This makes it a convenient tool for error-free improvisation.

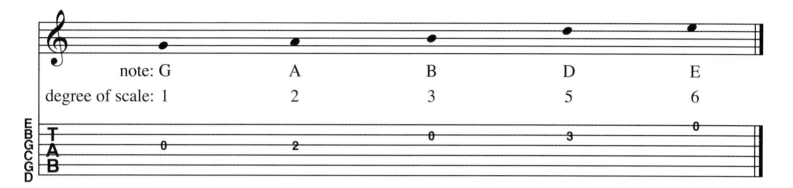

note:	G	A	B	D	E
degree of scale:	1	2	3	5	6

The black dots in the following diagram designate the G major pentatonic scale in the *G Kilauea* tuning.

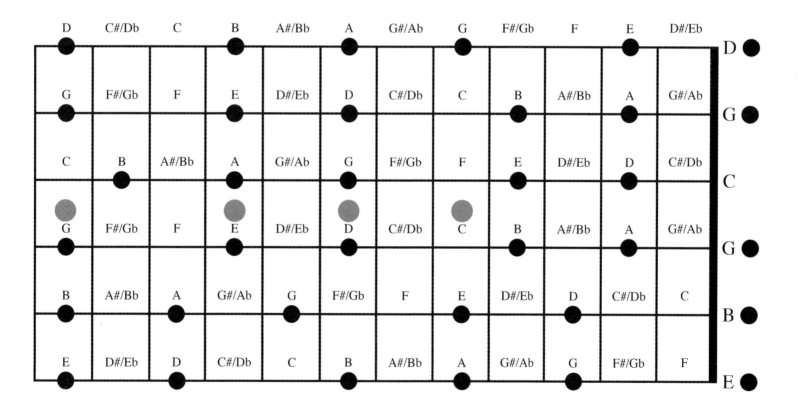

Thirds & Sixths

Thirds and sixths are indigenous intervals to guitar music. They are widely used in the compositions and improvisations of many genres, including Hawaiian slack key guitar. They play easily on the fretboard and are a quick solution to filling out single-note melody lines. The following charts show thirds and sixths in the key of G on the top three strings of a guitar. Note that the exact same positions are used in standard tuning and *G Kilauea* tuning because the top three strings of both tunings are G, B, and E.

Thirds on the 1st & 2nd Strings

Thirds on the 2nd & 3rd Strings

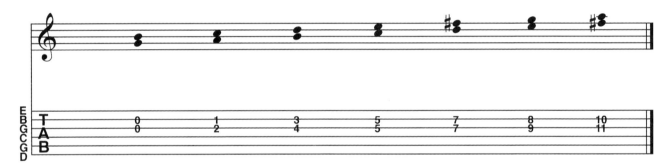

Sixths on the 1st & 2nd Strings

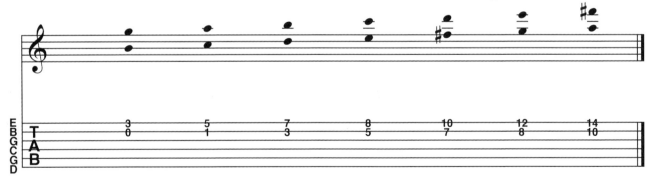

Sixths on the 1st & 3rd Strings

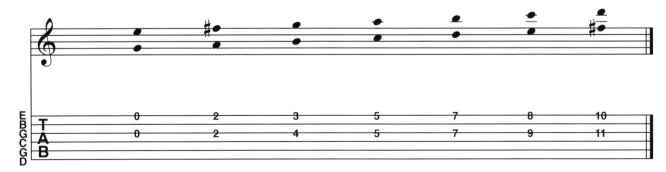

Chords in the Key of G Major

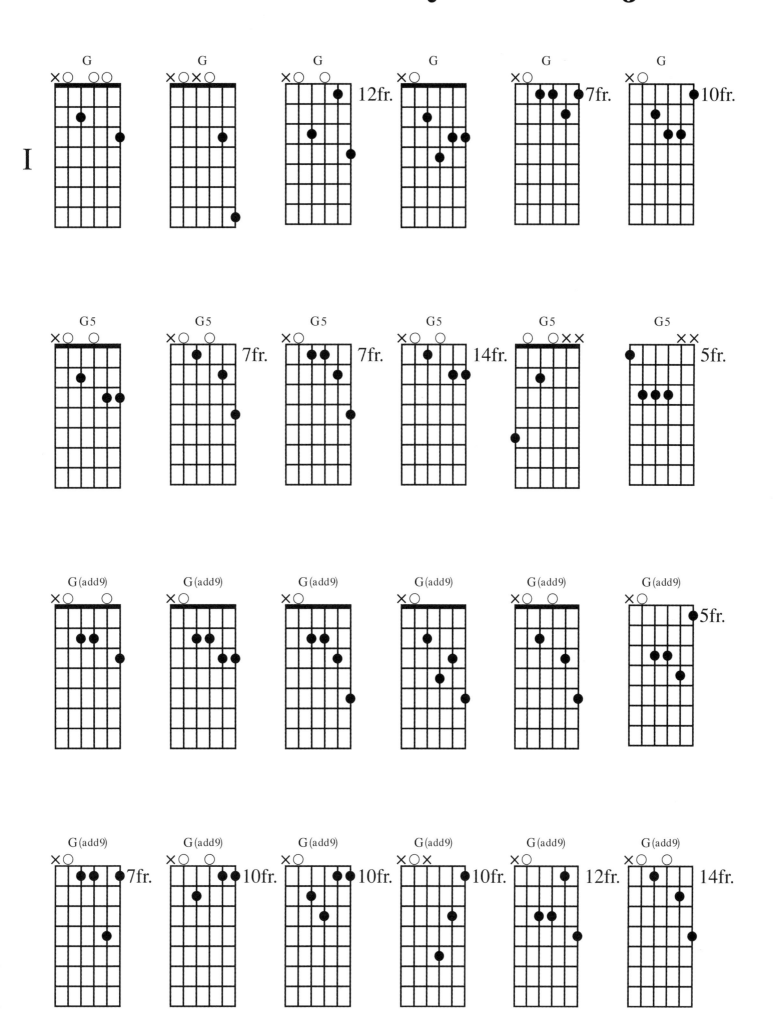

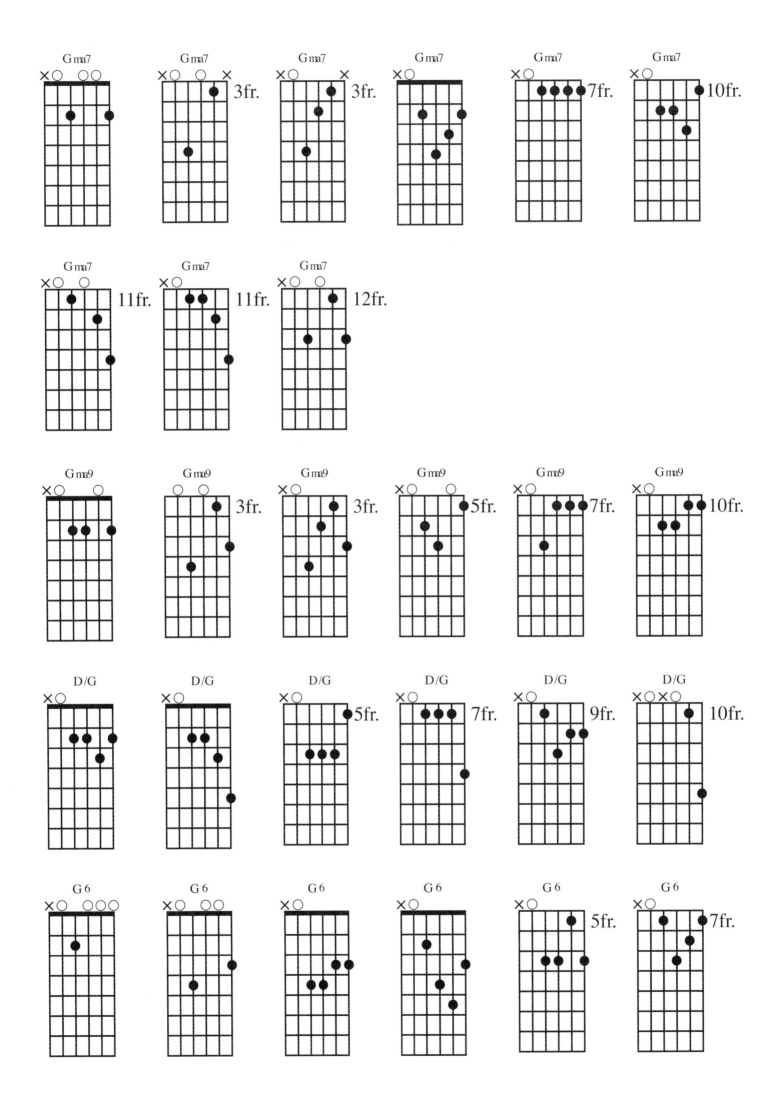

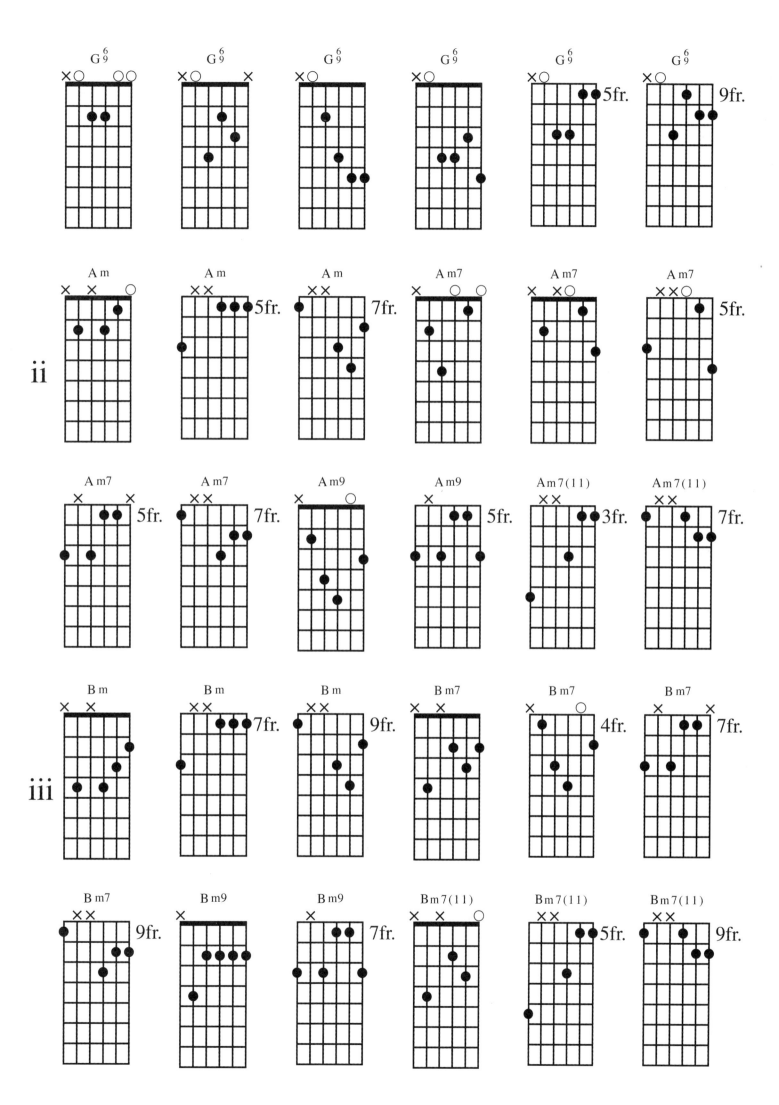

17

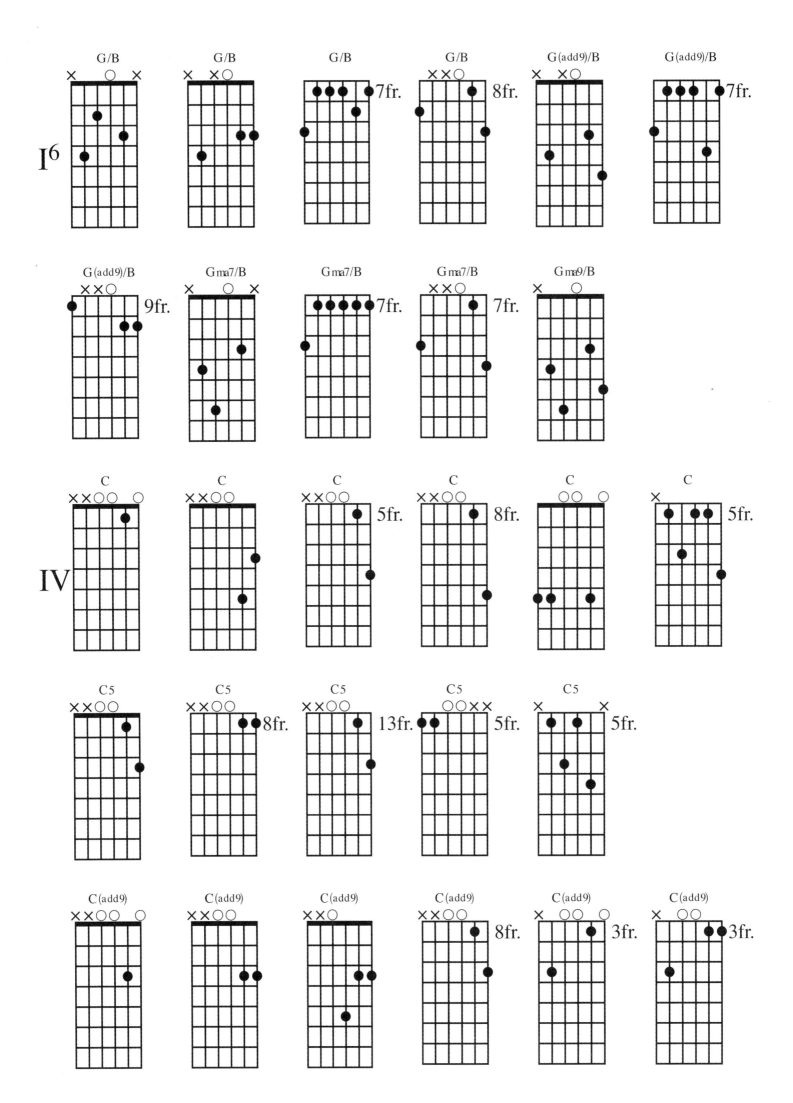

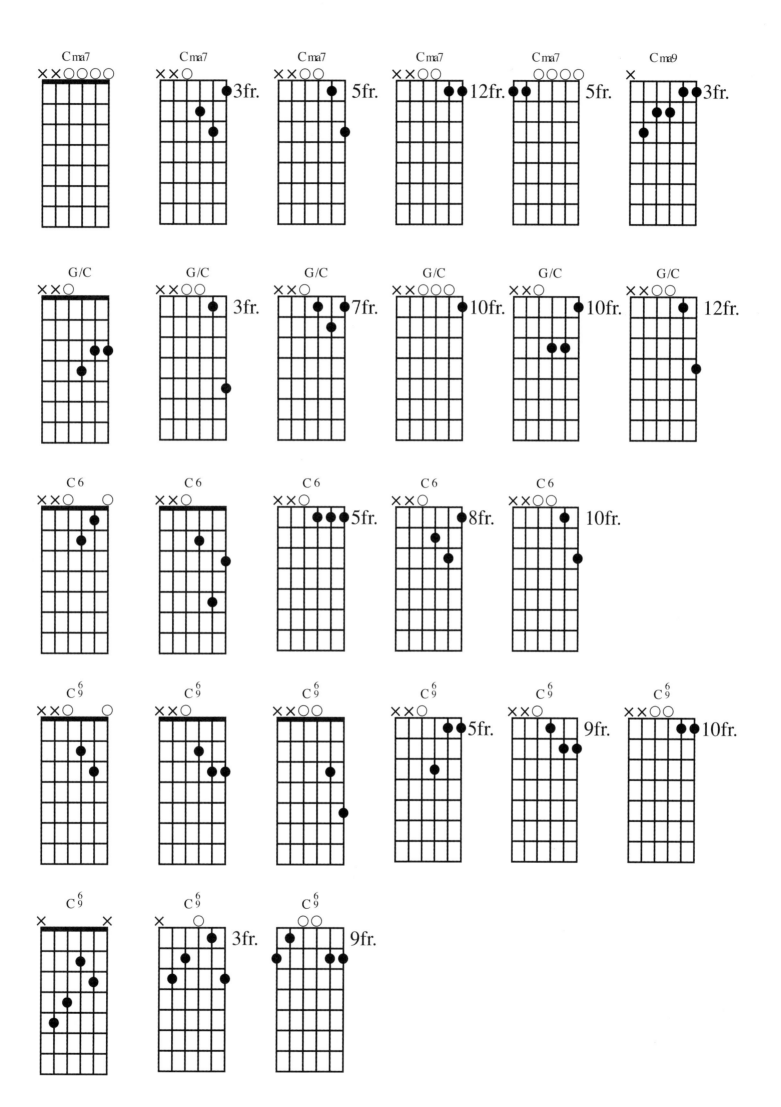

19

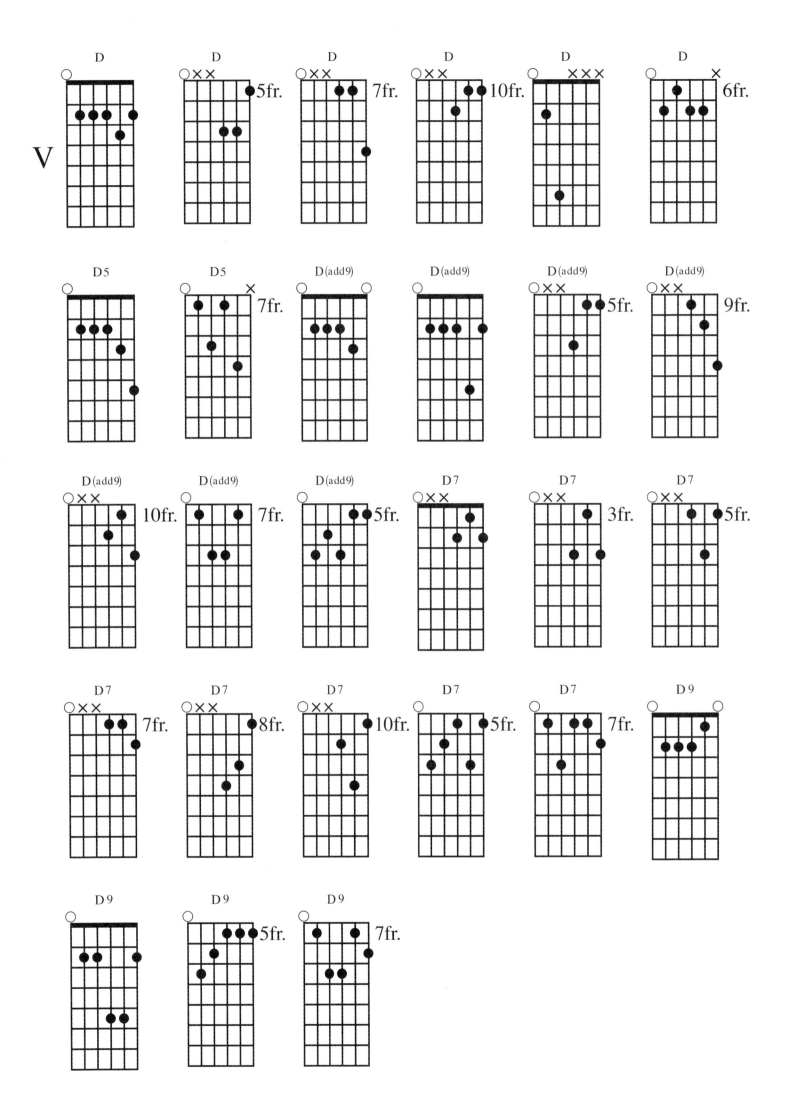

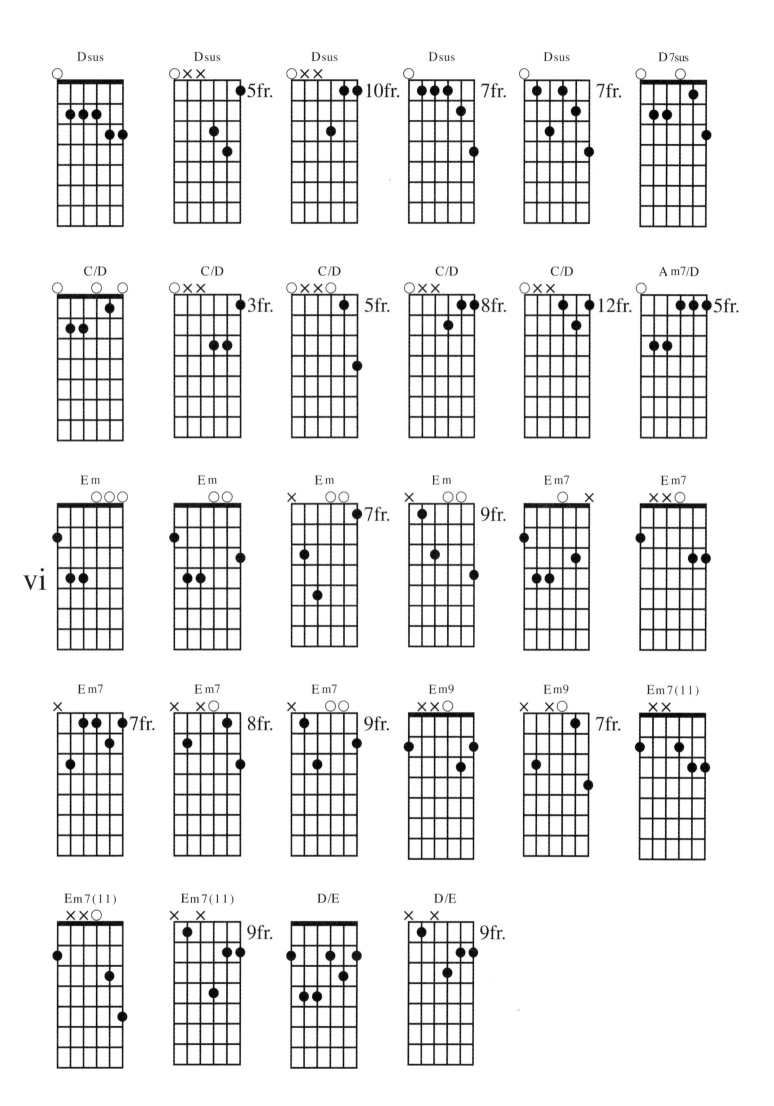

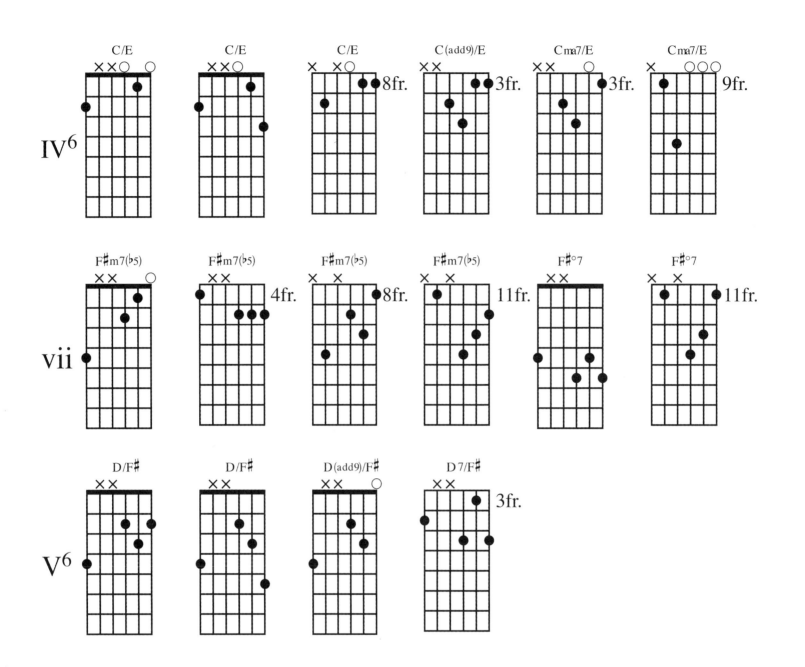

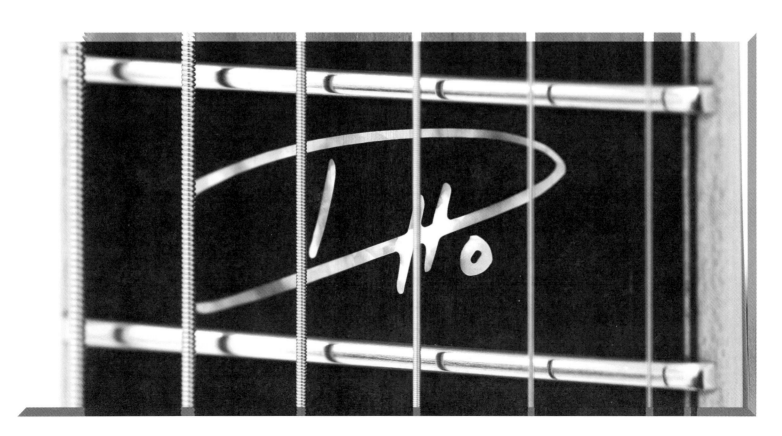

Arranging Concepts

Composing an original arrangement for guitar is somewhat of a three-dimensional puzzle. The instrument has a limited polyphony of six and offers multiple ways of playing a melodic passage or chord. Pitches are determined by four fingers on the left hand (limited by their reach) and aided by available open strings. Beyond the two-dimensional approach of simply playing melody and chords, this chapter outlines seven techniques that introduce a third dimension—that which makes a piece innovative and unique.

Motifs

A motif is a short melodic theme that recurs throughout a piece. Weaving an original motif into a piece ties it together and adds cohesion to an arrangement. It engages a listener when the melody is not active, and most importantly, this compositional element is an artistic signature—something no other arrangement of that piece would have.

In my arrangement of *Hawai'i Aloha*, I composed a three-note motif:

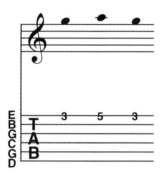

It is used as the theme of the introduction and a counterpoint to the melody throughout the piece. The subtle recurrences of the motif gradually raise awareness of its presence.

Measures 11-14 of *Hawai'i Aloha*

Ostinato

An ostinato is a repeating musical figure. Continual repetition gradually places it in the background of a listener's consciousness, allowing attention to be focused on elements that change such as the melody and harmony. It creates a subliminal energy.

I used an ostinato in my arrangement of *Pupu A'o 'Ewa*. It begins as the introduction and continues though the entire piece with the exception of the solo section. The greatest challenge of this arrangement was maintaining the ostinato, melody, and bass simultaneously.

Measures 5-8 of *Pupu A'o 'Ewa*

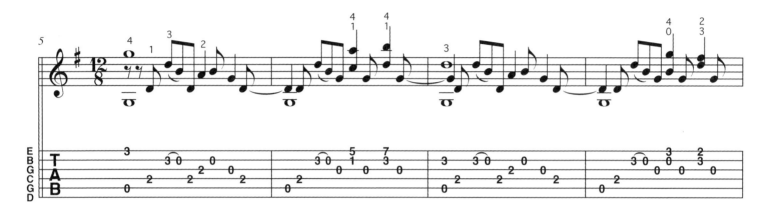

Pedal Point

This technique is traditionally defined as a low sustained note over which a passage is played. An inverted pedal point is a high sustained note or group of notes, and an internal pedal point is a sustained musical element in the middle register of a piece. Guitar strings do not sustain indefinitely, so it is often necessary to re-attack pedal points to sustain them through passages.

The following excerpt from *A World Away* is an example of an internal pedal point. The notes that are pedaled are G, C, and G, and they are played in a pattern that can also be considered an ostinato.

Measures 61-64 of *A World Away*

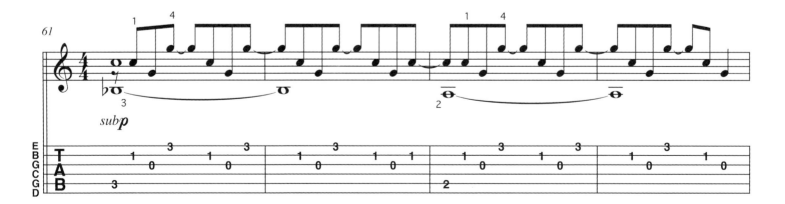

Contrary Motion

This can best be described as two musical elements that move in opposite directions. Well suited for piano, each hand would play a separate part as they move in contrary motion. On guitar, only one hand (the left hand) defines the majority of the pitches, making this technique exceptionally challenging.

This passage of *Hawai'i Pono'i* is a short example of contrary motion. I used it to build energy towards the end of the phrase.

Measures 13-14 of *Hawai'i Pono'i*

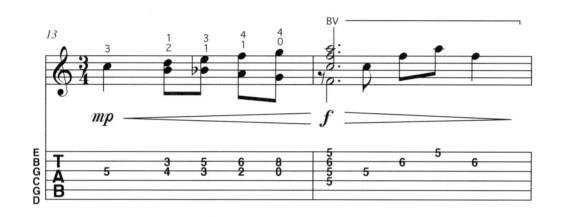

Parallel Motion

Unlike contrary motion, parallel motion is one of the most popular harmonization techniques on guitar. The most common intervals used in parallel are thirds, sixths, octaves, and tenths.

The melody of *Dreams of Eternity* is harmonized with sixths, which gives it fullness and brings it to the forefront of the musical texture.

Measures 1-4 of *Dreams of Eternity*

Oblique Motion

When one musical element remains constant in pitch while another moves, this is called oblique motion. It is an effective way to add interest to a static melody.

I treated some of the melody in *Hawai'i Pono'i* this way. Notice how an inner voice moves downward in a stepwise motion while the melody remains constant.

Measures 1-2 of *Hawai'i Pono'i*

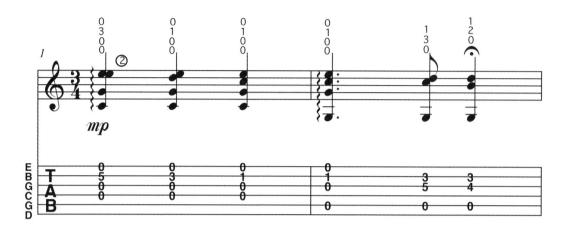

Reharmonization

Any melody can be harmonized in a number of different ways. Reharmonizing a piece maintains a listener's interest by changing the relationship between the melody and its supporting harmony.

An example of this can be found at the end of *Pomaika'i*, where the closing statement is repeated and reharmonized.

Measures 35-37 of *Pomaika'i*

Measures 40-42 of *Pomaika'i*

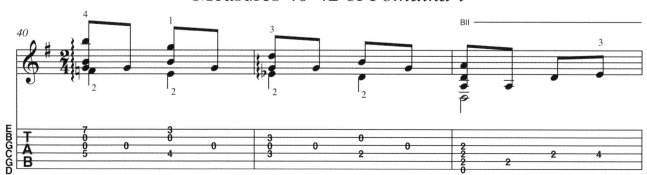

Allure of the Islands

♩ = 124

Daniel Ho

27

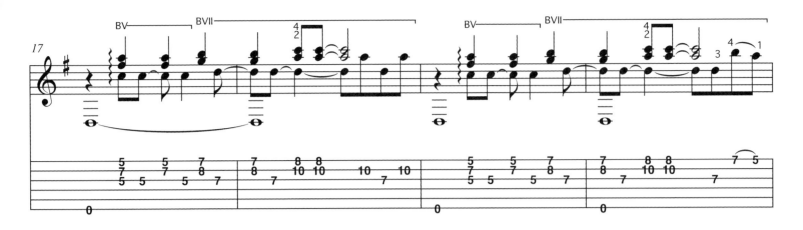

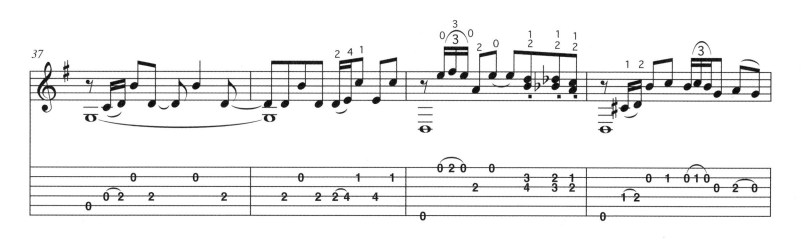

D. C. al Coda

dim.　　　　　rit.　　　　　　　　　　　　　　　　　　　　　　　　　　　　　*p*　　*fine*

Hawai'i Pono'i

Stately

Text by King David Kalakaua
Melody by Henry Berger
Arrangement by Daniel Ho

Aloha 'Oe

Composed by Queen Lili'uokalani
Arrangement by Daniel Ho

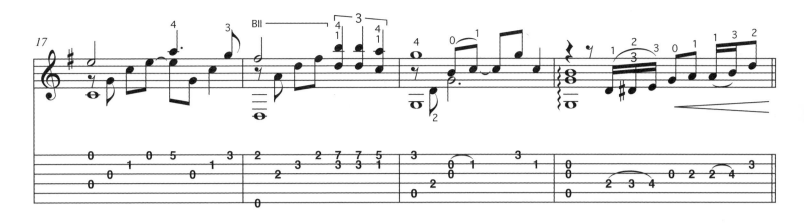

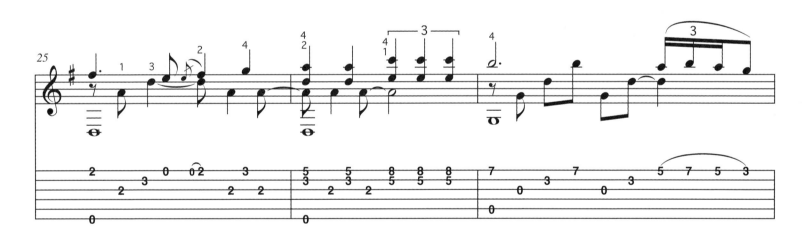

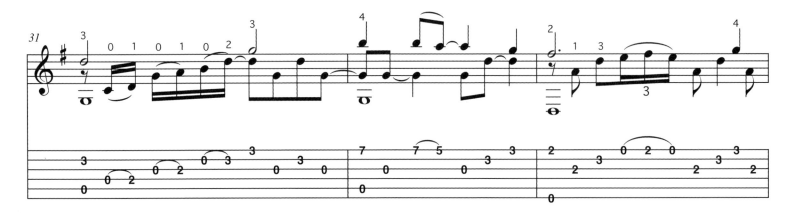

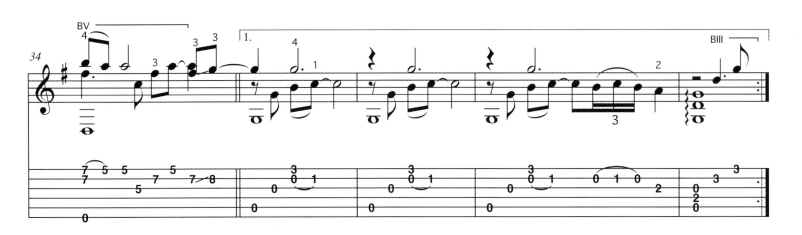

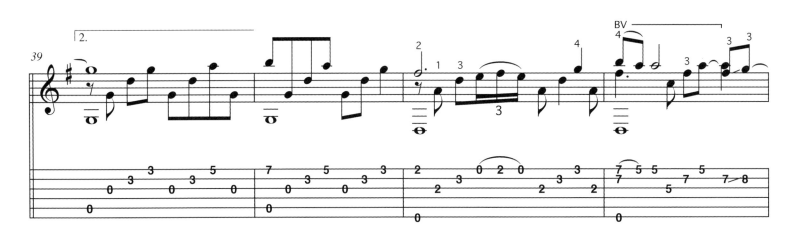

Pomaika'i *(the Blessing)*

Rubato

Daniel Ho

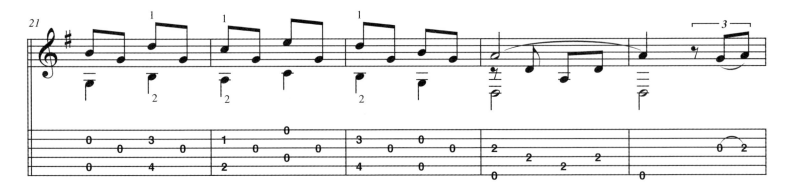

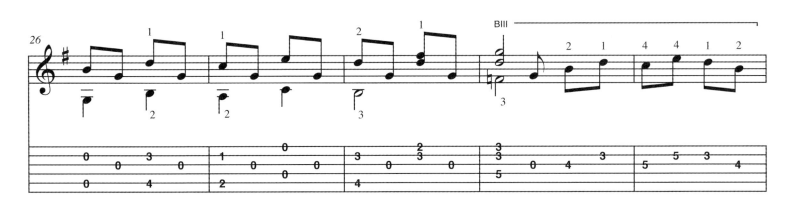

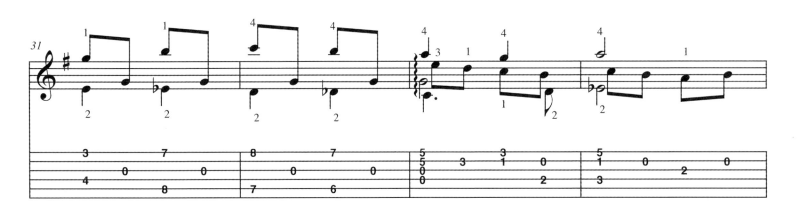

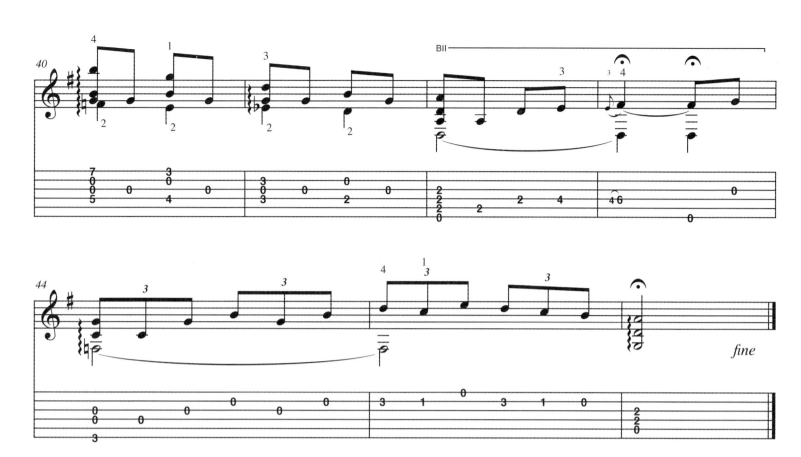

Dreams of Eternity

♩ = 128

Daniel Ho

38

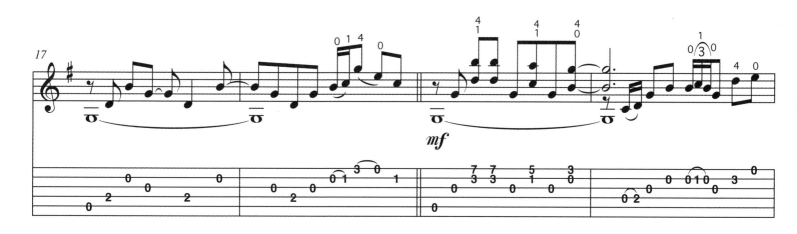
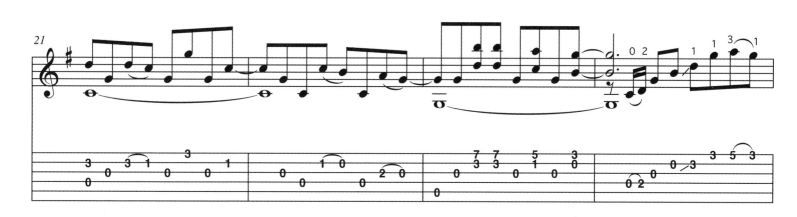
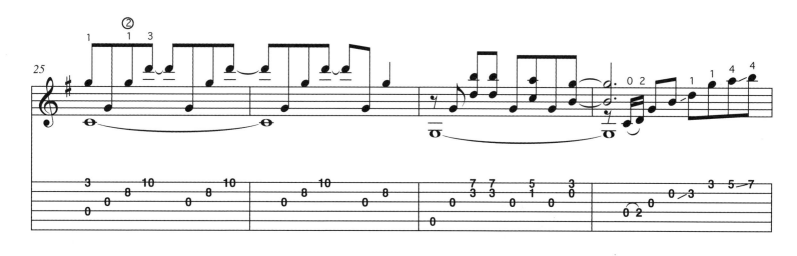

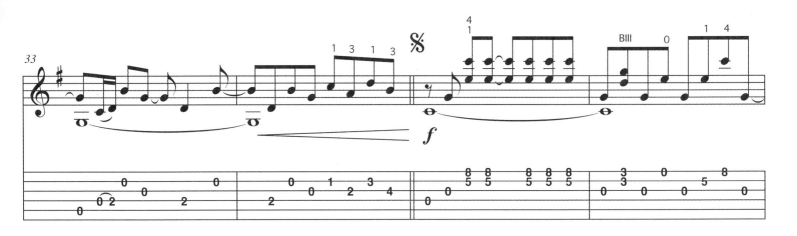

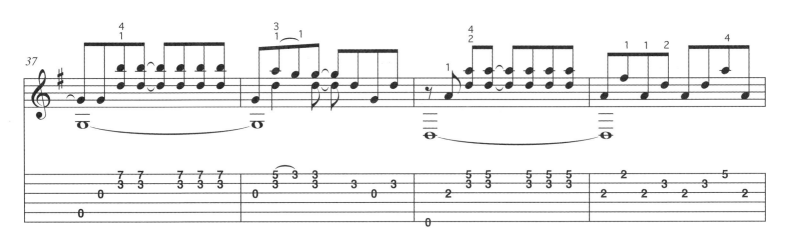

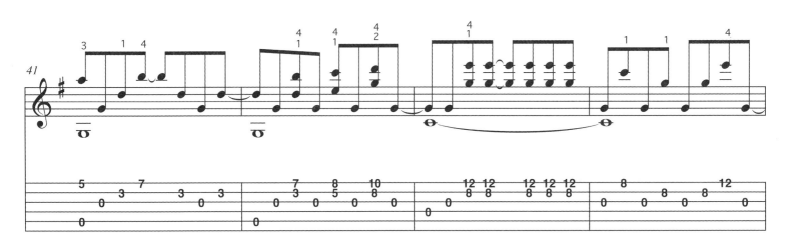

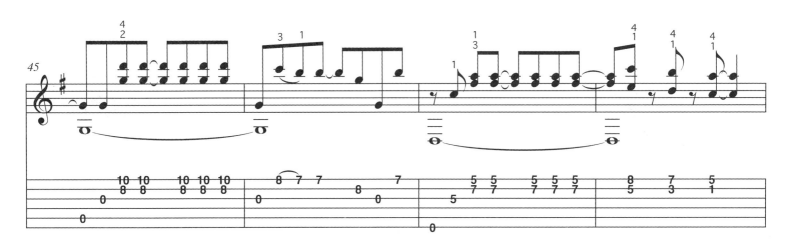

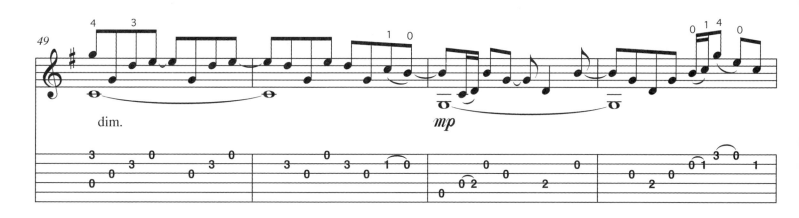

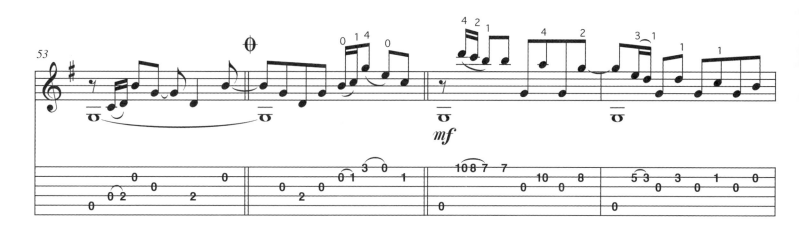

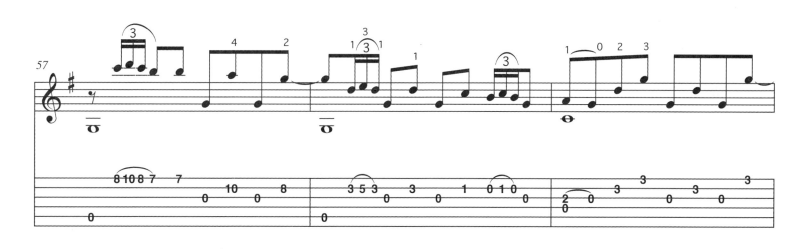

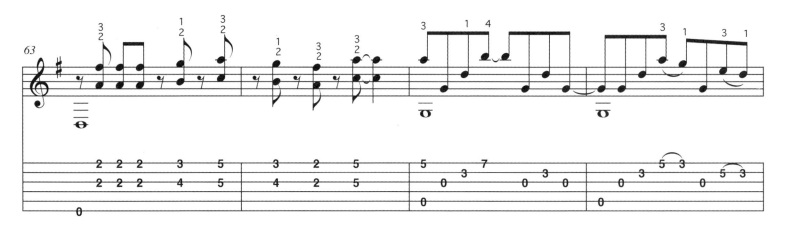

D. S. al Coda

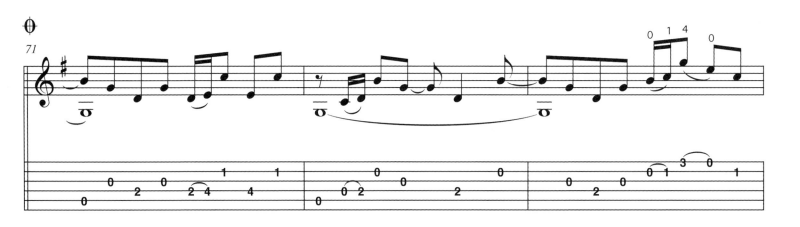

rit.

fine

42

Pupu A'o 'Ewa

Traditional
Arrangement by Daniel Ho

Kumu Mele *(Simple as a Sunrise)*

Daniel Ho

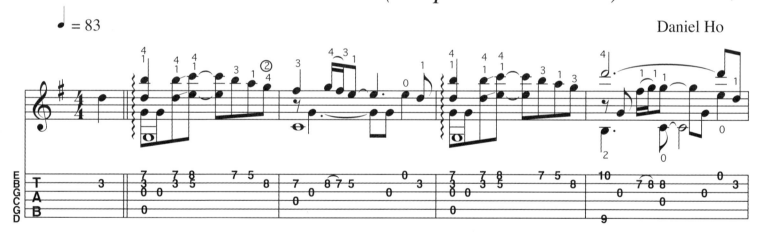

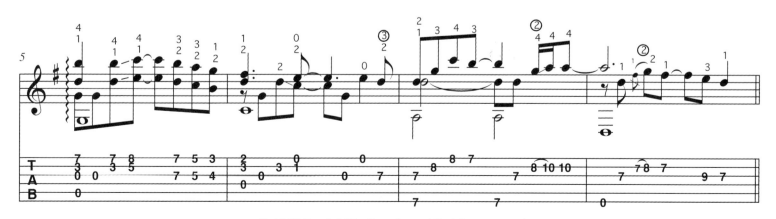

47

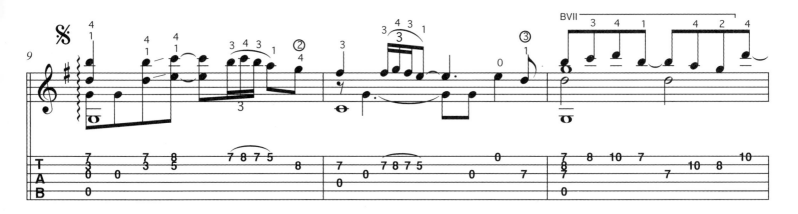

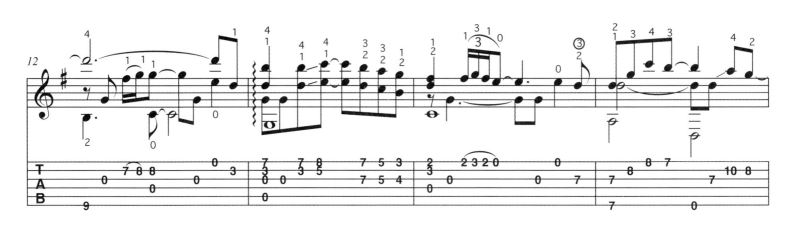

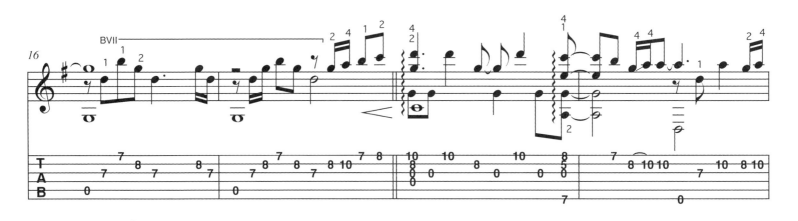

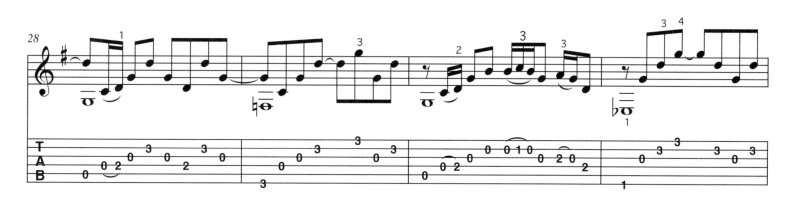
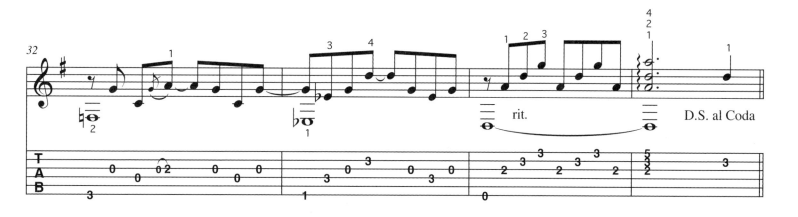

Maui Dawn

Hawai'i Aloha

Text by Lorenzo Lyons
Melody by James McGranahan
Arrangement by Daniel Ho

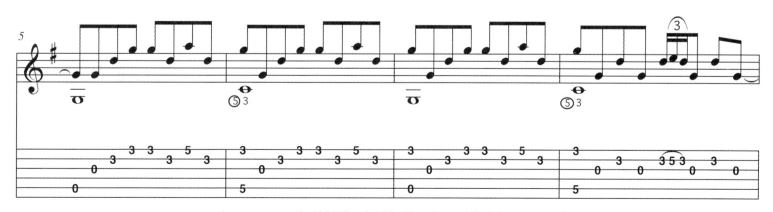

Lia

Daniel Ho

♩ = 102

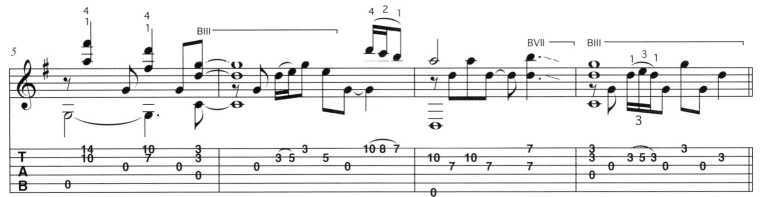

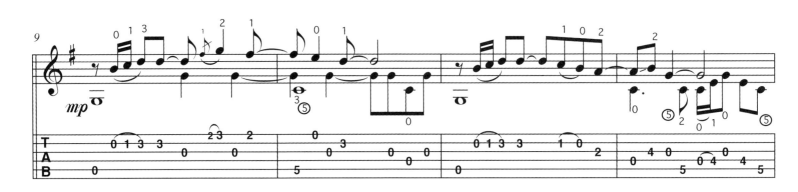

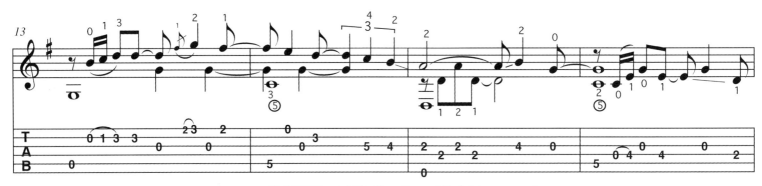

A World Away

Daniel Ho

64

Plantation Waltz

♩ = 152

Daniel Ho

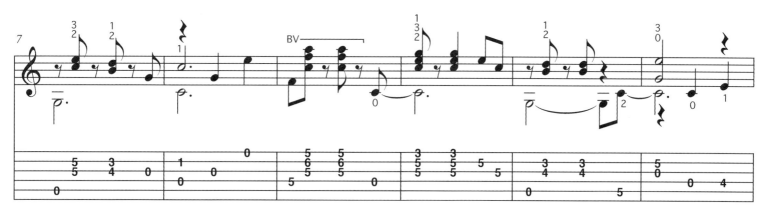

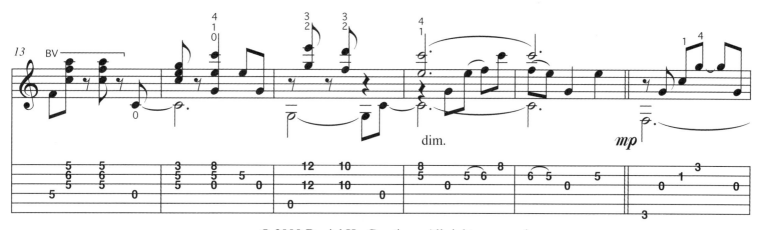

Slack Tides

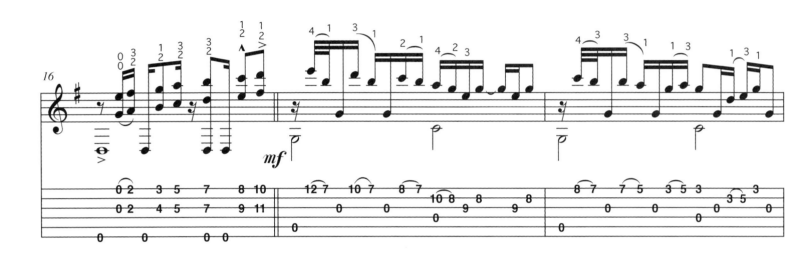

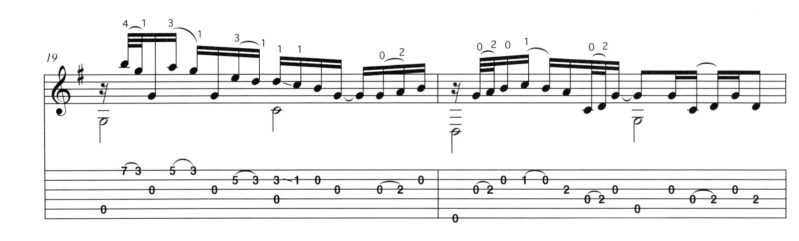

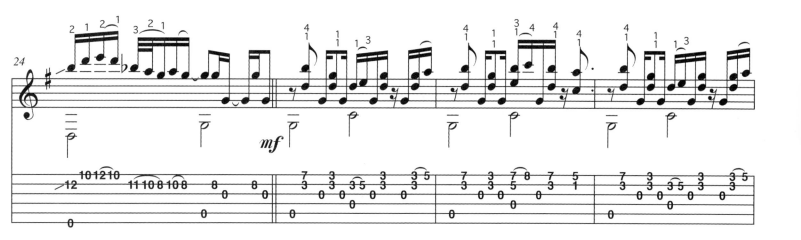

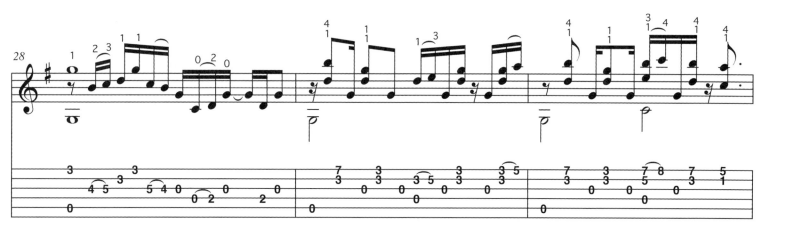

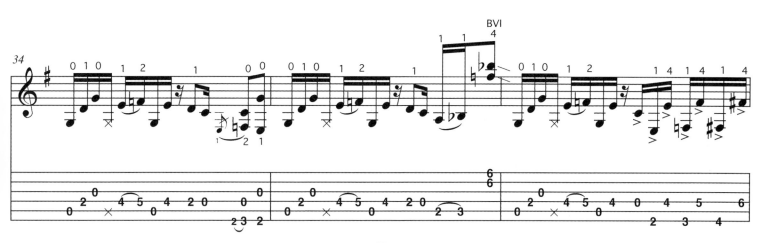

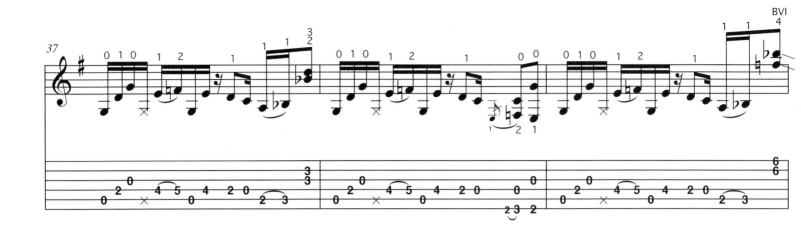

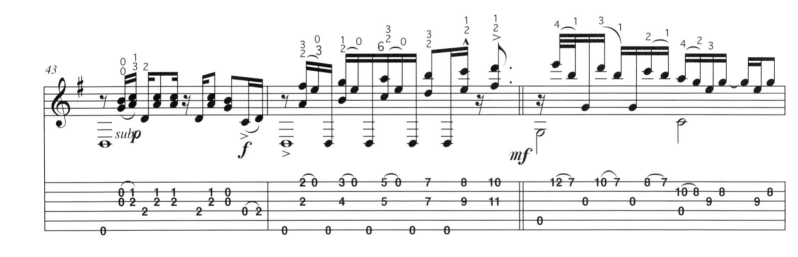

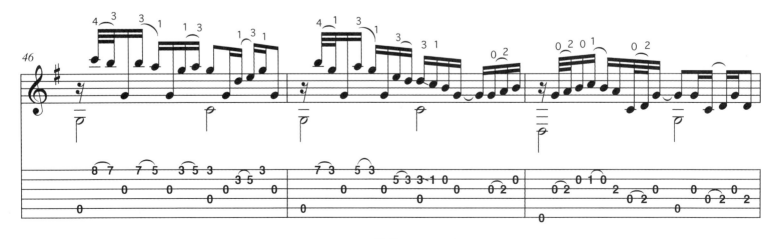

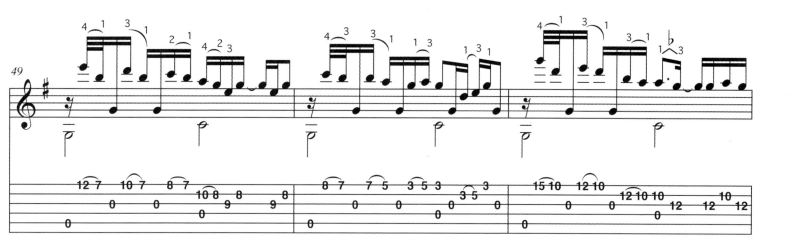

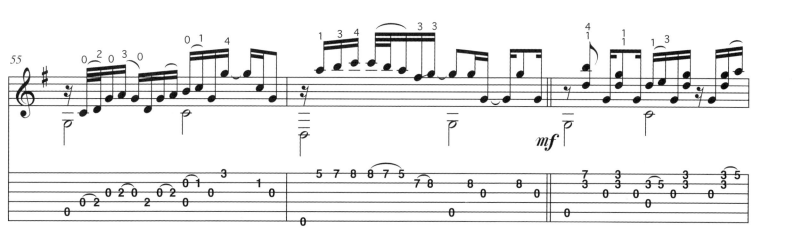
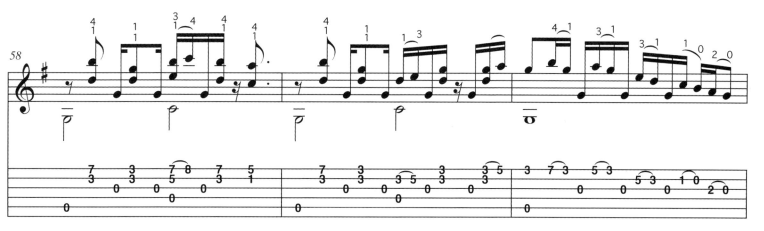

Song Credits

Allure of the Islands
Composed by Daniel Ho (© 1998 Daniel Ho Creations)
Recording: Hawaiian Slack Key Guitar, the Complete Collection

Hawai'i Pono'i
Text by King David Kalakaua, melody by Henry Berger
Arrangement by Daniel Ho (Arrangement © 1998 Daniel Ho Creations)
Recording: Hawaiian Slack Key Guitar, the Complete Collection

Aloha 'Oe
Composed by Queen Lili'uokalani
Arrangement by Daniel Ho (Arrangement © 1998 Daniel Ho Creations)
Recording: Hawaiian Slack Key Guitar, the Complete Collection

Pomaika'i *(the Blessing)*
Composed by Daniel Ho (© 2006 Daniel Ho Creations)
Recording: *see www.DanielHo.com for information*

Dreams of Eternity
Composed by Daniel Ho (© 1998 Daniel Ho Creations)
Recording: Hawaiian Slack Key Guitar, the Complete Collection

Pupu A'o 'Ewa
Traditional
Arrangement by Daniel Ho (Arrangement © 1998 Daniel Ho Creations)
Recording: Hawaiian Slack Key Guitar, the Complete Collection

Kumu Mele *(Simple as a Sunrise)*
Composed by Daniel Ho (© 1997 Daniel Ho Creations)
Recordings: Hawaiian Slack Key Guitar, the Complete Collection *(instrumental)*
Legends of Hawaiian Slack Key Guitar, Live from Maui *(live recording)*
Simple as a Sunrise *(vocal)*

Maui Dawn
Composed by Daniel Ho (© 1998 Daniel Ho Creations)
Recording: Hawaiian Slack Key Guitar, the Complete Collection

Hawai'i Aloha
Text by Lorenzo Lyons, melody by James McGranahan
Arrangement by Daniel Ho (Arrangement © 1998 Daniel Ho Creations)
Recording: Hawaiian Slack Key Guitar, the Complete Collection

Lia
Composed by Daniel Ho (© 1997 Daniel Ho Creations)
Recordings: Hawaiian Slack Key Guitar, the Complete Collection
Masters of Hawaiian Slack Key Guitar, vol. 1 *(live recording)*

A World Away
Composed by Daniel Ho (© 2000 Daniel Ho Creations)
Recording: Hawaiian Slack Key Guitar, the Complete Collection

Plantation Waltz
Composed by Daniel Ho (© 2000 Daniel Ho Creations)
Recording: Hawaiian Slack Key Guitar, the Complete Collection

Slack Tides
Composed by Daniel Ho (© 2000 Daniel Ho Creations)
Recordings: Hawaiian Slack Key Guitar, the Complete Collection
Masters of Hawaiian Slack Key Guitar, vol. 1 *(live recording)*

Selected Discography
Daniel Ho Creations

For current information, please visit: **www.DanielHo.com**

CD Title: Hawaiian Slack Key Guitar, the Complete Collection
Artist: Daniel Ho
Catalog Number: DHC 80428

CD Title: Simple as a Sunrise
Artist: Daniel Ho
Catalog Number: DHC 80005

CD Title: Masters of Hawaiian Slack Key Guitar, vol. 1
Artists: Various
Catalog Number: DHC 80007

CD Title: Legends of Hawaiian Slack Key Guitar, Live from Maui
Artists: Various
Catalog Number: DHC 80008

CD Title: Skies of Blue
Artist: Daniel Ho
Catalog Number: DHC 80040